AMERICAN WOMEN PILOTS OF WORLD WAR II

Karen Donnelly

The Rosen Publishing Group, Inc., New York

Published in 2004 by The Rosen Publishing Group, Inc.
29 East 21st Street, New York, NY 10010

Library of Congress Cataloging-in-Publication Data

Donnelly, Karen.
American women pilots of World War II/by Karen Donnelly.
    p. cm.—(American women at war)
Summary: Profiles American women who served as pilots during World
War II, and describes their struggles to prove their value both in wartime
and after returning home.
Includes bibliographical references and index.
ISBN 0-8239-4453-0 (lib. bdg.)
1. Air pilots, Military—United States—Biography—Juvenile literature.
2. Women air pilots—United States—Biography—Juvenile literature. 3. World
War, 1939–1945—Aerial operations, American—Juvenile literature. 4. United
States—Biography—Juvenile literature. [1. Air pilots, Military. 2. Women
Airforce Service Pilots (U.S.) 3. Women's rights—History. 4. Women—
Biography. 5. World War, 1939–1945—Participation, Female.]
I. Title: American women pilots of World War Two. II. Title: American
women pilots of World War 2. III. Title. IV. Series.
D790.D658 2003
940.54'4973'082—dc21
                                         2003011024

Manufactured in the United States of America

On the front cover: A group of women pilots from the Women Airforce
Service Pilots program during World War II sit around and do some "hangar
flying"—talking about their flying experiences.
On the back cover: A P-51 Mustang, one of the many aircraft types ferried
by women for overseas deployment.

Contents

INTRODUCTION

During the early years of aviation, Americans were entranced by airplanes. Families packed picnic lunches and took Sunday afternoon excursions to the nearest airport to watch the planes take off and land. Few people got a chance to fly in a plane. Many were afraid. Pilots, almost always men, were considered daring and courageous. Famous aviators like Charles Lindbergh and Amelia Earhart were celebrities, like rock stars and professional athletes are today.

In the late 1930s, war raged in Europe. Americans, though, did not want to become directly

involved in the conflict. Congress maintained a position of neutrality. America would not take sides in the war. Then on December 7, 1941, 360 Japanese planes attacked the U.S. military base at Pearl Harbor in Hawaii. More than 2,300 American soldiers, sailors, and civilians were killed. America could no longer stand on the sidelines. By December 11, President Franklin D. Roosevelt had declared war on Japan, Germany, and Italy.

Everyone was caught in a wave of patriotism. Citizens looked for ways to help their country fight. Young men joined the army. Women wanted to help, too. Many filled jobs in factories that had been left vacant by soldiers serving overseas.

Two women, Nancy Harkness Love and Jacqueline Cochran, had unique skills to offer their country. They were experienced pilots. They knew that the

A wartime poster by artist J. Howard Miller encourages women to show their strength and support the war effort.

Famous aviator Amelia Earhart strikes a pose in front of her aircraft before the flight over the Pacific Ocean in 1937 during which she disappeared. Earhart was an inspiration to many of the women who served as pilots during World War II.

U.S. government would not allow women to fly into combat. But they believed that women pilots could fly noncombat missions, like moving airplanes from a factory to an army base. They presented proposals to two different offices in the Army Air Force. Neither knew of the other's proposal. Nancy Love proposed hiring women with commercial pilot's licenses to ferry aircraft for the ferry commands. Jacqueline Cochran proposed training women pilots who had a private pilot's license to fly military aircraft. At the beginning of the war, the Army Air Force had enough male pilots and turned down the proposals. However, as the war progressed and male pilots were lost, the Army Air Force reconsidered its decision. Eventually, both proposals were accepted. Two separate groups of women pilots were formed as civil service employees. In 1943, they were merged into one group—the Women Airforce Service Pilots.

When the call went out, more than 25,000 women with flying experience responded. Of these, 1,102 would graduate from the training program to operational duty. Evelyn Sharp became one of the original members of the Women's Auxiliary Ferrying Squadron, Nancy Love's program. Dorothy Swain Lewis began as a flight instructor, teaching male pilots who would eventually need to land their planes on aircraft carriers. Ann Baumgartner Carl served as a test pilot, eventually becoming the first woman to fly a jet.

When the program was disbanded in December 1944, 916 women pilots were still in service. They did not want to go home. Congress had decided that male pilots should fill their cockpits. Many would never fly again. Their service to the country went unnoticed for years. Finally, in 1977, President Jimmy Carter signed a bill that gave veteran status to the women pilots who had served in World War II.

NANCY HARKNESS LOVE

On a hot summer day in 1935, sixteen-year-old Nancy Harkness was enjoying a horseback ride in a field outside her hometown of Houghton, Michigan. She heard an unusual sound and looked to the sky. A shiny sleek airplane circled overhead, then landed nearby. The pilot was a barnstormer who made his living giving rides in his plane. Harkness paid $5 for a short flight. That night at dinner, she told her father that she had decided to quit high school and become a pilot.

Harkness's father suggested that she take flying lessons while she was in school. Nancy agreed

and spent the last weeks of August logging as
many hours in the air as possible. On August 31,
she soloed (flew alone) for the first time. In
September, she returned to her boarding school,
Milton Academy, near Boston, Massachusetts.

She continued to fly while at Milton Academy
and, afterward, at Vassar College in Poughkeepsie,
New York. In New York, she spent weekends at
the airport. She earned extra money by taking students for rides in an airplane that she rented.
Before she was twenty years old, she earned her
commercial license and her transport pilot's
license. Unfortunately, Harkness's time at Vassar
was cut short. Financial trouble caused by the
Great Depression forced her to leave school. She
got a job as the Boston-area sales representative
for Beechcraft, a manufacturer of small planes
based in Wichita, Kansas.

Selling airplanes, though, was not nearly as
exciting as flying them. So Harkness was thrilled
when in 1935 Phoebe Omlie, special assistant for
intelligence of the National Advisory Committee
for Aeronautics, chose her to work with President
Franklin D. Roosevelt's Work Progress
Administration's Airmarking Project. In the 1930s,
pilots navigated by landmarks on the ground that

Nancy Harkness Love first suggested to the Army Air Corps that women pilots be used to ferry aircraft for the military. She had earned her commercial pilot's license before she was twenty years old.

they could recognize from the sky. Through the Airmarking Project, the roofs of prominent buildings were painted with markers and the name of the town in which they stood. Harkness traveled the eastern part of the United States convincing town leaders to participate in the project. Later, women pilots ferrying planes across the country would use these markers to find their way.

In 1935, Harkness left her job to care for her ailing mother and to plan her wedding to Robert Love, an Army Air Corps Reserve officer. Bob had been a student at Princeton and the Massachusetts Institute of Technology but left school to start his own company, Inter City Airways, at East Boston Airport.

Inter City had also undertaken an important role in the developing war in Europe. The company ferried airplanes from the United States to Canada. These planes would eventually be sent to England to help defend against the Germans. Harkness's flight on a ferrying mission for Inter City gave her an idea. She knew of at least forty-nine women pilots qualified for the same job. On May 21, 1940, she wrote to Colonel Robert Olds of the Army Air Corps Plans Division, suggesting that women pilots be used to ferry aircraft for the military.

In 1940, though, the war was still being fought in Europe. The United States was not directly involved. Colonel Olds did not totally refuse Harkness's proposal. He kept it on file without acting on it. Then on December 7, 1941, the Japanese attacked Pearl Harbor, bringing the United States into the war. Suddenly the need for trained pilots increased dramatically.

After Pearl Harbor, all airports along the East Coast were shut down, including Boston-area airports, grounding Inter City Airways. Bob Love was placed on active duty with the Air Transport Command (ATC), headquartered in Washington, D.C. In 1942, he and Nancy moved to Washington, where she found a job working in the Baltimore, Maryland, office of the ATC's Ferrying Command.

Surprisingly, war rationing made it easier for Harkness to get gasoline for an airplane than for a car. So she commuted the 60 miles (96.6 kilometers) from Washington to Baltimore each day by plane. At the same time, Colonel William Tunner, commander of the ATC, was on a desperate hunt for pilots. When he heard from Bob Love that his wife was a pilot, the idea of using women on ferrying missions was reborn. A few days later, Colonel Tunner met with Harkness. She drafted a new

proposal that he submitted to Brigadier General
Harold George.

Harkness's proposal included hiring women on
the same basis as men—with the same qualifications,
at the same salary, and with the same training program. The ATC, however, imposed more restrictions
on women, requiring more flying time and a high
school diploma. Even though Harkness agreed, making her women pilots more qualified than many
men, women were still able to fly only the smallest
airplanes. In addition, the women would be
restricted to one ferry base in New Castle, Delaware,
rather than combined with squadrons of male pilots.

Another snag would prove to be an even bigger
problem. Harkness, General George, and Colonel
Tunner assumed that women, like men, would be
hired as civilians, trained for ninety days, and
then commissioned into the Army Air Force
(AAF). By June, the AAF had a women's auxiliary,
the Women's Auxiliary Army Corps (WAAC).
Harkness proposed that pilots could be part of
this organization. Unfortunately, the laws estab-
lishing the WAAC did not provide flight pay or
flying officers. Women pilots could not be commissioned until Congress passed a new law, a
process that could take months.

Colonel Tunner needed pilots so badly, he asked Harkness to move ahead even though the future of the program was uncertain. She agreed, promising an initial squadron of twenty-five pilots. Women would be hired as civil service employees. They both hoped that Congress would act as soon as possible to amend the WAAC legislation.

On September 5, the Women's Auxiliary Ferrying Squadron (WAFS) was activated with twenty-eight-year-old Nancy Harkness Love as director. She immediately sent telegrams to eighty-three experienced women pilots. On September 10, Secretary of War Henry Stimson publicly announced the program. Women who had not received telegrams responded when newspaper and magazine articles reported that women pilots were being recruited to serve their country.

At about the same time, Jacqueline Cochran was named director of a training program for women pilots, called the Women's Flying Training Detachment (WFTD). The WFTD was separate from the WAFS. Women pilots with many hours of experience would fill the first WAFS squadron, but more pilots would be needed. The WFTD would train those pilots.

RUTH LAW

During World War I, aviator Ruth Law offered her services as a pilot to the Army Signal Corps. Instead, the government sent her around the country to recruit male pilots and raise money for war bonds. Women were considered too high-strung for wartime flying.

Ruth Law poses in an early Wright flyer. In 1916, Law set an American aviation record by flying cross-country nonstop for 590 miles (950 km). After World War I, she formed Ruth Law's Flying Circus, a three-plane troupe that amazed spectators at state and county fairs by racing against cars, flying through fireworks, and setting altitude and distance records.

On October 19, 1942, seven women from the WAFS, in addition to Harkness, completed the training program and began ferrying planes. On October 22, six of the new graduates received their first ferrying assignment. They were to deliver Piper Cubs from the factory in Lock Haven, Pennsylvania, to Mitchel Field on Long Island, New York.

By December 1942, the army's ferrying demands had increased. Pilots were needed to fly bigger, faster, and heavier planes. A single squadron of women pilots in Delaware was no longer sufficient. Harkness knew that additional WAFS units should be formed at other bases. She traveled the country evaluating other bases where male ferrying squadrons were located. She chose Dallas, Texas; Romulus, Michigan, outside Detroit; and Long Beach, California.

Harkness wanted to prove that women could fly the new, bigger airplanes. What better way to do this than to fly the planes herself? She had her sights set on the P-51 Mustang, one of the fastest airplanes ever built. Because her first flight in the P-51 would be solo, she would need to rely on her own past experience and her instincts. She taxied down the runway and felt the plane lift off the

A B-17 "Flying Fortress" crosses the United States. Many of these bombers, used with great effect against the Germans in Europe, were ferried from their assembly plants to England by women pilots.

ground. She soared 10,000 feet (3,048 meters) over the Pacific Ocean. Yes, she could handle this plane. Her WAFS could, too.

During the first six months of 1943, she "checked out" (flew successfully) in cargo planes, bombers, and attack planes. Then she got a call from Colonel Tunner at Ferrying Division Headquarters in Cincinnati, Ohio. He wanted her back at headquarters.

The summer of 1943 would be a "hot" one. Jacqueline Cochran continued to fight for control

of all women pilots. She was not satisfied as
director of the Women's Flying Training
Detachment. In July, her office moved from Fort
Worth, Texas, to the Pentagon in Washington, D.C.
She was named director of women pilots with the
Army Air Force. At the same time, Harkness was
appointed executive for the WAFS. In August, the
Ferrying Division announced that all women pilots
would serve under a new organization—Women
Airforce Service Pilots (WASP)—and that
Jacqueline Cochran would be its director.

Colonel Tunner continued to support Harkness
and her ferrying squadron of women pilots. He
called her into his office and offered her the
chance to fly a B-17, called "the Flying Fortress,"
to England. Until then, women pilots had been
restricted to domestic flights, within the borders of
the United States. To prepare for the flight, she
would need advanced training, including night flying, night landing, and instrument operations.
Betty Gillies, an original member of the WAFS,
was also part of the training. She would be copilot.

On September 2, Harkness and Gillies began
their trip. They flew from Cincinnati to Presque
Isle in Maine. On September 3, 1943, they landed
in Goose Bay, Labrador, Canada, planning to

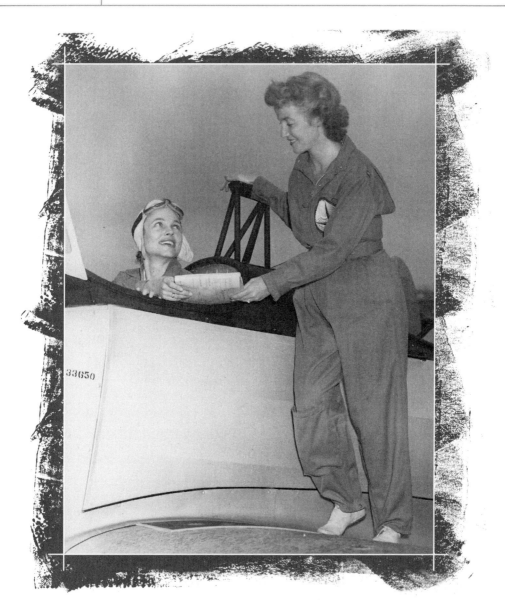

Nancy Harkness Love of the Women Airforce Service Pilots stands on the wing of a trainer with her first student, Betty Gillies. In 1943, Harkness and Gillies tried to ferry a B-17 to England, but General Hap Arnold, afraid of the adverse publicity if women were killed in combat, replaced them with a male pilot.

leave for Prestwick, Scotland, the next day. Unfortunately, General Hap Arnold learned of the mission, and Harkness and Gillies were grounded. General Arnold ordered their plane reassigned to a male pilot. He was afraid of the publicity that would result if women pilots were killed in a war zone.

Harkness and Gillies returned to domestic ferrying missions. By October 1944, 130 women pilots ferried two-thirds of all pursuit aircraft manufactured in the United States. They flew the planes from their factories to the airfields from which they would leave for locations overseas. The women were surprised and hurt, then, when General Arnold announced that the WASP would be deactivated. Harkness had heard talk of deactivation but believed that her ferrying squadrons would be protected.

Harkness's hopes were dashed, however. The letter delivered on October 8 was sent to all WASP, including those in the ATC's ferrying group. Between October and December 20, the date of deactivation, the women pilots took Harkness's advice. They flew any kind of airplane they could get their hands on.

On December 19, thirty-eight WASP gathered in Wilmington, Delaware, one last time. They

toasted each other's accomplishments at the
Officer's Club. Then they returned to their barracks to pack for the trip home. Ironically, that
night the Officer's Club caught fire and burned to
the ground.

Nancy Harkness Love and the WASP felt
betrayed. They had been told that their contribution to their country was vital. Suddenly, they
were tossed aside. Harkness left in a C-54 four-
engine transport plane, ferrying it to California.

Her flying days were not yet over, however.
Colonel Tunner had been transferred to Calcutta,
India. He commanded the ferrying division that
supplied the Chinese army's fight against Japan by
flying over the Himalayas and the jungles of
Burma. Tunner asked that Harkness be assigned to
his division. Her work was largely administrative,
interviewing pilots and staff. She took side trips to
China and the Assam Valley in India and returned
home in January 1945. In 1946, she was awarded
the Air Medal by General Harold George and a
citation signed by President Harry Truman.

After the war, Harkness had three daughters
and helped her husband with his airplane and
boating business. In 1952, she and her family
moved to Martha's Vineyard, an island off the

coast of Massachusetts. She continued to fly, taking her daughters to doctor and dentist appointments by air. She died at age sixty-two on October 22, 1976, one year, one month, and one day before the bill giving veteran's status to the WASP would be signed by President Jimmy Carter.

The first women accepted into the WASP knew that more than their own success was at stake. Most people, even other women, believed that "girls" were too small and frail to handle the controls of a combat airplane. If this group of women pilots failed, they failed as women, not as individuals. The struggle to be accepted for their talent and ability rather than dismissed because of their gender would continue for decades. Claire Booth Luce, on being appointed United States ambassador to Italy by president Dwight D. Eisenhower in 1953, said, "Because I am a woman, I must make unusual efforts to succeed. If I fail, no one will say, 'She doesn't have what it takes,' They will say, 'Women don't have what it takes.'"

JACQUELINE COCHRAN— THE BEGINNING

Jacqueline "Jackie" Cochran was probably born near Muscogee, Florida. She grew up living with a foster family who told her she was born sometime in May. They all agreed that May 11 would be the day, but the year remained a mystery. Her life in Florida sawmill towns was harsh. Her family lived on the verge of starvation. Until she was eight years old, she had no shoes.

Because her family was so poor, Jackie had only two years of formal education. Her teacher, Miss Bostwick, though, became one of the biggest influences on Jackie's life. Miss Bostwick

saw a special spark in this wild, scrubby child. She gave Cochran the first new dress she owned—not a hand-me-down. More important, Miss Bostwick taught Jackie to read.

When Jackie was eight years old, her family moved to Columbus, Georgia, to work in the local cotton mills. She became self-supporting, working a twelve-hour shift for six cents an hour. At the end of her first week, she used her salary to buy her first pair of shoes.

The cotton mill closed when the labor union called a strike. Cochran found a new job working for the owner of a beauty shop. By the time she was thirteen years old, she had learned to cut and style hair. She also learned to give a permanent wave, a new process that took all day.

Near age eighteen, Cochran decided to apply for nurses' training. After finishing her studies, she worked in the office of a local doctor. She discovered, however, that life as a mill-town nurse was sad. The families she served suffered the same hard life she had escaped. She chose to begin a new life in Pensacola, Florida.

In Pensacola, Cochran became a partner in a beauty shop. Soon, though, she was ready for bigger things. She sold her share of the shop to her

partner and moved to New York City. She found a
job at Antoine's salon in Saks Fifth Avenue.
Antoine also had a salon in Miami and soon she
was spending the winter months there. In 1932, at
a dinner party in a Miami hotel, she met Floyd
Odlum, who at age thirty-six had become a self-
made millionaire. She told him that she had been
considering starting her own business, a company
selling cosmetics. She thought it would give her a
chance to travel. Odlum gave her advice that
changed her life. He suggested that she could
reach more customers if she learned to fly an airplane. Floyd Odlum's relationship with Cochran
did not end with that advice. He also would
become her husband on May 10, 1936.

Once Cochran had her pilot's license, she was
not content to use it simply to sell cosmetics. In
1937, after Amelia Earhart had disappeared,
Cochran entered the Bendix International Air Race.
She won the women's purse and finished third,
ahead of most male competitors. She continued to
race, setting speed records. On December 4, 1937,
she raced from New York to Miami in four hours
and twelve minutes, setting a national record.

Because of her racing success, Cochran had
become the new American air heroine. This

brought her to the attention of Alexander de Seversky, an aircraft designer who had immigrated to the United States from Russia. He had designed a sleek pursuit plane with a 1,000-horsepower engine, the P-35. He wanted to sell it to the Army Air Corps, but had been unsuccessful. He asked Cochran to fly his plane in the next race, demonstrating its speed. She agreed. Before the race,

In 1938, aviator Jacqueline Cochran won the Bendix International Air Race in a prototype of what was to become the P-47 Thunderbird. Cochran was instrumental in convincing the armed forces to use women pilots to ferry aircraft overseas for the war effort.

Seversky added a new design innovation. Cochran's plane would have extra fuel tanks built into the wings so that she could fly the race nonstop.

On September 3, 1938, spectators crowded the Cleveland Municipal Airport, anticipating the arrival of the first Bendix racer. At 2:23 PM, Cochran's P-35 swooped across the finish line. She won the 2,042-mile (3,286 km) race in eight hours, ten minutes, and thirty-one seconds. The second racer, forced to land in Wichita to refuel, would not arrive for another hour.

Although Cochran did not know it, she had made her first contribution to the war effort. The Army Air Corps wanted Seversky's plane. The P-35 became the P-47 Thunderbird fighter, a pursuit plane used by the Allies in Africa and Europe. Soon Cochran's influence would become more dramatic.

In September 1939, Poland surrendered to the German army. Jackie Cochran wrote a letter to First Lady Eleanor Roosevelt, suggesting that women pilots could play an important role in the military, flying noncombat missions. Cochran was available to begin the necessary planning. The Army Air Corps, however, was not ready to send women into the air.

In March 1941, the United States was still officially neutral, not an active participant, in the war in Europe. President Franklin D. Roosevelt, however, found a way to help Great Britain. He asked Congress to pass the Lend-Lease Act, which allowed the United States to "lend" supplies, like tanks and airplanes, to the Allied forces. American pilots flew planes to Canada. The British Air Transport Auxiliary (ATA) had the responsibility of getting the planes to England.

At an awards luncheon, Cochran discussed the British ATA's problem with General Hap Arnold of the U.S. Army Air Corps and Clayton Knight, who directed the American recruiting effort. They were desperate for pilots. British women pilots were already serving. General Arnold suggested that Cochran contact ATA headquarters in Montreal and volunteer her services.

Cochran was thrilled to have a chance to participate in the war effort. In June, she completed her flight test in Montreal and was ordered to ferry a Lockheed Hudson from Montreal to Prestwick, Scotland. The ATA pilots in Montreal objected. They worried that the ATA would be blamed for her possible death. As a compromise, ATA command decided that Cochran's male copilot would handle the takeoff and landing. She would pilot the plane across the Atlantic. On June 17,

Cochran and her crew took off from Montreal.
Twelve hours later, they landed in Scotland.

Cochran did not just make the flight to deliver
her plane. She also wanted to see how the British
ATA worked. In July 1941, she became a tactical con-
sultant, working with Colonel Robert Olds. Cochran
and her staff of seven researchers checked 300,000
files at the Civil Aeronautics Administration (CAA).
They found 2,733 female licensed pilots, 150 with
more than 200 hours of flying experience, enough to
qualify as commercial airline pilots. Cochran sent
them all a questionnaire asking if they would be willing to fly for their country during a war. More than
130 pilots responded. Yes, they were ready.

In July 1941, Cochran submitted a proposal to
General Arnold for an "Organization of a Woman
Pilot's Division of the Air Corps Ferrying
Command." At the time, however, General Arnold
did not see a reason to use women pilots because
there were enough male pilots. He spoke to
Cochran and suggested that she accept the British
ATA's request to recruit women pilots for duty
overseas. Cochran accepted that challenge, promising the ATA to recruit 125 women pilots with
300 hours of flying experience. She had a difficult
time. The women pilots were required to commit

to an eighteen-month overseas contract. Some had families with small children and were unwilling to leave them behind. Many believed that if the British used women pilots, then eventually the American government would, too. Cochran had to assure her ATA recruits that the U.S. military had refused her proposal and had no intention of using women pilots in the near future. General

General Hap Arnold and his aides. Arnold eventually agreed to the creation of the Women Airforce Service Pilots group, and Jacqueline Cochran was put in charge of organizing the training.

In October 1942 First Lady Eleanor Roosevelt *(right)* talks with some of the women pilots who ferried combat aircraft to England.

Arnold directed the Ferry Command not to hire women pilots until Cochran had fulfilled her agreement with the British.

Then, on December 7, 1941, the Japanese attacked Pearl Harbor. World War II was no longer the European War. President Roosevelt declared war on Japan. On December 11, he declared war on Germany and Italy. Suddenly, the need for American combat pilots became critical.

In the spring of 1942, Cochran went to England to oversee the arrival of the first group of the twenty-five American women pilots who she recruited for the ATA. By late August, the last recruits would be sworn into service. General Arnold visited Cochran in London. He told her that soon women pilots would also be needed in the United States. He would soon need her back to take on this task.

While Cochran was in England, however, Nancy Harkness Love spoke with Colonel William Tunner and General Harold George. Without discussing the plans with General Arnold, on September 10, Secretary of War Henry L. Stimson announced the formation of the Women's Auxiliary Ferrying Squadron with Harkness as director.

Cochran was furious and, recently returned from England, stormed into General Arnold's office. On September 15, the War Department announced the formation of a second group of women pilots, a training group. This second program, to be directed by Jacqueline Cochran, was called the Women's Flying Training Detachment.

JACQUELINE COCHRAN— THE WASP

In October 1942, the United States Army Air Force announced the start of a training program for women pilots. Jackie Cochran was flooded with at least 25,000 applications. She and three assistants traveled around the country, giving interviews, arranging medical examinations, and making final decisions. Out of the 25,000, Cochran planned to train about 1,000 pilots.

To get her first training class in the air, Cochran needed a base from which to operate. In November, she chose Aviation Enterprises, Ltd., located at Howard Hughes Field at Houston

Municipal Airport in Texas. Rooms in local tourist motels served as housing. The trainees traveled from the motels to the airfield in army supply semitrailer trucks. The women sat on wooden boards built into the backs of the trucks.

The biggest problem was finding airplanes for the women to fly. Army trainer aircraft were on order but had not yet arrived. Cochran and the training command took control of almost every private plane between Fort Worth and Houston.

Clothing was another problem. The trainees had not been promised uniforms. They brought with them whatever flying clothes they had used at home. Some women went to nearby department stores, bought men's trousers, and had them altered. Finally, in mid-December, the ninety trainees then stationed in Houston were excited when a pile of GI flying suits arrived. But their joy was short-lived. The khaki GI jumpsuits were men's sizes. The shoulders and pant legs were so large that the women nicknamed them "zoot suits." To wear the suits, the women had to roll up the sleeves and pant legs and tie a belt around the waist.

Cochran was not happy with the Houston airfield. She wanted a location that could be developed

In July 1943, women ferry pilots were causing enough excitement to make the cover of *Life* magazine. It was the Japanese attack on Pearl Harbor in December 1941 and the resulting need for more pilots that broke resistance in the military to female aviators.

FIFINELLA

Walt Disney designed Fifinella, the female flying gremlin that became the emblem of the WASP. Male gremlins, it seems, were invisible, mischievous creatures capable of causing mechanical failure and other unexplained problems. They were often accused of playing unpredictable pranks on pilots. Fifinella, a female gremlin, flew from the clouds to chase away the tricksters and keep the WASP fleet flying.

---

into a permanent training center, handling classes of more than 125 pilots. The British were giving up their base in Sweetwater, Texas. Cochran arranged to take it over, naming her new base Avenger Field. In March 1943, she instructed the Houston trainees to pack their belongings and ferry themselves and their airplanes to Sweetwater.

The new facility was not fancy, but it was an improvement over Houston. Eight huts served as barracks. They were divided into six-woman bunkrooms called bays. A longer building housed classrooms and the "ready room," where pilots waited their turn to fly. Each day, half the

Under a sign featuring the flying gremlin Fifinella, designed by Walt Disney, three women pilot recruits enter Avenger Field to begin their training.

trainees were in class; the rest were in the air or waiting to fly. A control tower and a hangar were under construction.

Word of the all-women facility spread quickly to other bases. "The first week the girls were at

Sweetwater we had over one hundred men pilots make 'forced landings' on the field," Cochran wrote in her autobiography *The Stars at Noon*. "The field was barred both by gate and from the air except in real emergency." As a result, Avenger Field became known as Cochran's Convent.

A graduation ceremony for women pilots at Avenger Field near Sweetwater, Texas, the airfield where Jacqueline Cochran trained her WASP pilots

JANET HARMON BRAGG

In 1933, Janet Bragg, an African American, lived outside Chicago, where she worked as a nurse. She began flying lessons but found them too expensive. She decided to buy her own plane and rent it to other pilots to help cover the cost. All African American pilots, male or female, were hampered by racial discrimination. Most airports were "white only." Bragg and her fellow pilots started their own airport in Robbins, Illinois, 20 miles (32 km) southwest of Chicago, and formed the Challenger Aero Club. In 1939, they opened the Coffey School of Aviation, eventually participating in the Civilian Pilot Training Program. Bragg attempted to join the WASP, interviewing in 1942. At that time in Sweetwater, Texas, restaurants and hotels were segregated. Bragg was denied entrance because there would be no place for her to stay. Already fighting prejudice against women pilots, Jacqueline Cochran was not ready to take on racial prejudice as well.

Cochran, though, did not spend much time at Avenger Field. Her office was in the Pentagon, and from there she handled administrative tasks. She spent a great deal of time trying to make the WASP part of the military. She also flew back and forth, checking on the assignments of her WASP graduates. Of course, she participated in the graduation of each class.

At the first graduation, the women pilots were dressed in khaki pants and blouses they had bought themselves. General Arnold, also present at the ceremony, suggested to Cochran that the "girls" deserved uniforms. Cochran agreed. She went to Bergdorf Goodman's in New York City and paid to have a uniform designed. The "Santiago Blue" suits were stylish, sophisticated, and professional. She also continually worked to expand the WASP program by arranging new work for them to do. Unlike Nancy Harkness, Cochran was not satisfied with a ferrying squadron. She arranged for her WASP to fly tow-targets, a dangerous mission that male pilots disliked. Gunners on the ground and in tanks fired at target flags that were attached to the tail of the plane. A few WASP even flew as test pilots.

Cochran could see, however, that her most important job was to get military status for the

Jacqueline Cochran, in the center of the photograph, visits one of the groups of women pilots being trained at Avenger Field.

WASP. Initially, the Army Air Force assumed that the WASP would become part of the WAC (formerly the WAAC), which was already militarized. Cochran, however, knew that if her pilots were WACs, she would lose control of her program.

Cochran hoped Congress would pass a bill giving the WASP military status. On February 19, 1944, the bill was introduced. The opposition, however, was ready. The civilian pilot training program had already been shut down, leaving its male instructors without flying jobs. Also, at this time, many people still believed that women belonged at home. Yes, they had been helpful, filling in for men who were not available. But now that men were ready to take over, the women should willingly give up their seats in the cockpits. Many articles in newspapers and magazines supported this view. "The arguments in Congress against the continuation of my training and flying program were strange," wrote Cochran in *Jacqueline Cochran: The Autobiography of the Greatest Woman Pilot of Aviation History*. "We were putting male pilots on bread lines, we were teenaged schoolgirls, stenographers, clerks, beauticians, housewives, and factory workers piloting military planes in a startlingly invalid program, we were wasting millions

JACQUELINE COCHRAN'S RECORD

1938   First woman to win the Bendix Trophy Race.

1950   Received the Harmon Trophy in 1950 as the Aviatrix of the Decade.

1953   Became the first woman to exceed the speed of sound.

1962   Established sixty-nine intercity and straight-line distance records for Lockheed in a Jet Star. She also was the first woman to fly a jet across the Atlantic Ocean.

1964   Set the record for a 100-kilometer (63-mile) course with a speed of 1,302 mph (2,095 km/h).

---

of taxpayer dollars to train women in a frivolous program . . . All of it was demoralizing and so very destructive of the truly heroic dimensions to which the WASPs had risen." Public support of the WASP was overwhelmed by rumors that women pilots did not really care about serving their country. They wanted to keep flying because they found it glamorous.

Of course, flying for the military was not really glamorous. It was dangerous, hard, sweaty work. But people did not understand this because the WASP had been kept isolated. Most Americans had not even known the program existed. Cochran had never tried to gain public support for her program. Letters opposing the WASP militarization flooded Congress. Cochran, however, refused to allow any member of the WASP to write to her senator or representative. She also forbade any WASP member to go to Washington. Some family members wrote on behalf of the WASP, but their words were not enough. On June 21, 1944, Congress defeated the bill to militarize the WASP.

The defeat of militarization did not eliminate the WASP program. Public opposition to the program was growing. Cochran prepared an extensive public report outlining the accomplishments of the WASP. Although the press reported the information, detailing how the women pilots were serving the war efforts, Cochran was fighting a losing battle.

On October 3, 1944, WASP across the country received letters announcing their deactivation on December 20. Jacqueline Cochran, however, would not be deactivated. She continued to fly, setting records and receiving awards. In 1971, she became the first living woman enshrined in the National Aviation Hall of Fame. She died in 1980.

EVELYN SHARP

In 1935, during the height of the Great Depression, John Sharp owned a restaurant and boardinghouse in Ord, Nebraska. One of his roomers, Jack Jefford, had opened a flying school. The Depression meant fewer people could afford the luxury of flying lessons, making it difficult for Jefford to pay his room and board. Sharp could not simply ignore the debt, but did not want to force Jefford to close the school. They struck a deal. Jefford would give flying lessons to Sharp's daughter, Evelyn, working off his debt in trade. Without realizing it, John Sharp had changed the

Three members of the Women Airforce Service Pilots, photographed at Long Beach, California *(from left to right):* Barbara Towne, Evelyn Sharp, and Cornilia Fort. Evelyn Sharp came into the program after accumulating more than 3,000 hours of flying time as a barnstormer.

direction of his daughter's life forever. Soon, she would become a celebrity, earning her living and supporting the Sharp family as a flight instructor and barnstormer. Then she would serve her country as the youngest member of the Women's Auxiliary Ferrying Squadron (WAFS).

The circumstances of Sharp's early life make her rise to celebrity even more surprising. She was born in Melstone, Montana, on October 20, 1919, to Orla and Elsie Crouse. Their wedding had been arranged quickly when they discovered that Elsie was pregnant. The marriage soon ended in divorce, leaving Elsie with a difficult choice. She would be unable to care for a baby alone. She arranged for John and Mary Sharp to adopt her baby. On December 2, 1919, Evelyn Genevieve Sharp became the legal daughter of John and Mary Sharp, moving with them to Kinsey, Montana.

When she was three years old, Evelyn and her family moved to Nebraska. Like most families during the Depression, John and Mary Sharp worked hard and suffered financial setbacks. They operated a grocery store and boardinghouse. They tried their hand at farming outside of Hastings, Nebraska. When the farm failed, the Sharps moved to Ord.

On February 4, 1935, Jack Jefford made the first payment on his debt to John Sharp. Evelyn had her flying lesson. On November 9, 1936, she passed her flight test, becoming a licensed private pilot. She was able to fly any single-engine airplane and take passengers for pleasure.

Just as her career appeared to be taking off, Sharp found herself grounded. Jack Jefford had closed his flying school and moved to Hastings. John Sharp, however, found a way for Sharp to fly. He convinced local businessmen to sponsor her. The men purchased a plane for her to fly. She became a celebrity, bringing publicity to Ord. The fees charged for rides generated income.

Sharp finally was able to support herself and her family doing what she loved. She crisscrossed the country, giving flight demonstrations, barn-storming shows, and pleasure rides. At the same time, the mood in the country was changing. The war in Europe was on everyone's mind. Sharp wanted to use her flying skills to help. In June 1940, she moved to Spearfish, North Dakota, to be an instructor for the Civilian Pilot Training Program (CPTP). She taught for the CPTP until December, and then moved to California to work as a flight instructor there.

On September 5, 1942, Sharp was one of eighty-four women who received a telegram inviting them to Wilmington, Delaware, to apply for the Women's Auxiliary Ferrying Squadron. To be eligible for the program, women pilots needed to meet stiffer requirements than male pilots. Men pilots could be between the ages of nineteen and forty-five. Only women ages twenty-one

The examining board for the Women Airforce Service Pilots program, which includes Nancy Harkness Love, questions Helen Mary Clark (*second from left*) about her flight experience.

to thirty-five were eligible. Women needed 500 hours of flying time, men only 200. Women needed a high school diploma; men needed to have completed only three years of high school. Men were trained as civilians for ninety days and then were commissioned into the Army Air Force. Women would remain civilians unless Congress passed a new law. Also, women were paid $250 a month; men were paid $380.

Sharp went to Wilmington, Delaware, where she passed her interview and flight test. She was accepted on October 20, 1942. She moved to New Castle Army Air Base (NCAAB) and into Bachelor's Officer Quarters 14 (BOQ 14), which had recently been vacated by its male residents. Teresa James, another WAFS recruit, described the conditions in BOQ 14 in *The Originals: The Woman's Auxiliary Ferrying Squadron of World War II*: "Our new home was built from two-by-fours, planks and boards. One window per room, two if you had a corner room . . . I never expected to see such a barren structure, because I had been informed that the men who had occupied BOQ 14 had moved to another building. I . . . was astonished at the sunlight peeking through the cracks in the walls . . . I picked out a room with the least daylight peeking through the cracks. Furnishings consisted of one sagging cot and one iron chair."[1]

The building had a common bathroom. The shower stalls had no curtains, and the toilets were out in the open. Modesty would become a thing of the past. Because many buildings at NCAAB were under construction, the ground was a sea of mud. To avoid sinking to her ankles, Sharp had to walk across planks from the road to the building. She paid seventy-five cents a day for this housing she lived in at BOQ 14 during her thirty-day training period. During that time, she spent twenty-five hours flying and seventy-two hours at ground school. By November 1942, she had completed her training and was eligible to wear the WAFS uniform: a belted jacket, matching shirt and slacks, and an overseas cap. Unlike male pilots who were officially part of the military, she had no clothing allowance and had to pay for her uniform.

Sharp's first assignment as a member of the WAFS was to fly one of ten new PT-19As from their factory in Hagerstown, Maryland, to Riddle-McKay Army Primary School in Union City, Tennessee. She and nine other WAFS rode a train to Maryland where they were stranded for days, waiting for miserable weather to clear. After they safely delivered the planes, their orders were to return as quickly as possible to NCAAB. Unfortunately, they were not allowed to hitch rides on any military planes piloted by men. No hint of scandal could be allowed to tarnish the WAFS reputation. When she returned to Wilmington, Sharp was handed a new set of orders. She reported to Lock Haven, Pennsylvania, and flew from there to Fort Smith, Arkansas. This would become the pattern of her early life with the WAFS: a train ride to pick up the plane; the delivery flight, weather permitting; and a train or bus ride back to base.

During the winter, these flights were a bone-chilling event. The PT-19As had open cockpits. Dressing to survive the freezing wind was the most important preparation. Sharp wore woolen under-wear under her uniform. She wore a leather-covered, fleece-lined, two-piece garment, and a pair of leather-covered, fleece-lined flying boots weighing about 15 pounds (6.8 kg). She added a fleece-lined helmet; a fleece-lined face mask with holes for eyes, nose, and mouth; goggles with fleece around the edges of the eyepiece to pro-tect her face from metal; and fleece-lined flying gloves. In addition, she carried a 25-pound (11 kg)

Pilot Alberta Kinney of the Women Airforce Service Pilots is seen here in full flying gear. In the unpressurized cockpits of the time, keeping pilots warm at high altitudes was a serious concern. Fleece-lined leather jackets and pants became standard flying gear.

At Avenger Field, two WASP trainees learn how to put on a parachute. By World War II, the parachute was standard emergency equipment for fighter pilots. But even with a parachute, pilots who had to bail out of damaged aircraft had to struggle to exit the plane without getting hung up on wreckage and to open their chutes in time. Computer automation and ejector seats make this process easier for modern pilots.

parachute. Also, she had to strap her navigational charts to her leg. Otherwise, the charts would likely blow out of the cockpit.

By early 1943, the twenty-eight original members of the WAFS had finished training. They were divided among four locations and were eventually joined by women graduating from Jacqueline Cochran's WASP program. Sharp was assigned to Long Beach Army Air Base in California. Soon after she arrived, restrictions that had kept women from flying larger, heavier planes were lifted. Sharp would be able to fly twin-engine cargo planes and pursuit aircraft, cruising at about 250 miles per hour (402 km/h).

At the end of September, Sharp was transferred to Palm Springs, California, where she became commander of the Twenty-first Squadron. Suddenly, in November, she was transferred back to Long Beach. Palm Springs had been designated a pursuit training school, but she was not chosen for the first class.

Back at Long Beach, Sharp began training for instrument flying. She wanted to fly more sophisticated aircraft and would need to be able to navigate without using landmarks on the ground. At Long Beach, a Link Trainer, a simulator, allowed pilots to practice instrument "flying"

HOLLYWOOD AND THE WOMEN PILOTS

In September 1943, Hollywood descended on the Long Beach Army Base to film *Ladies Courageous*, a movie that told the story of women pilots. However, the film, starring Loretta Young, Diana Barrymore, and Richard Fraser, depicted the pilots as more interested in gossip and romance than flying. Those who knew the real story, especially the pilots themselves, were angered and embarrassed. Also, because it was released in 1944, the movie may have helped convince Congress to vote down militarization for the women.

A Hollywood publicity photograph from the film Ladies Courageous *shows actress Loretta Young playing a WASP pilot.*

without leaving the ground and risking the danger of getting lost or crashing. As she felt more comfortable, Sharp also practiced in real flight. She passed the first of three instrument flight checks in January 1944 and the last on March 29, 1944.

The next day, she climbed into a "Lightning" P-38J destined for Newark, New Jersey. Fog forced her down in Palm Springs, where she spent the night. On March 31, she flew across Arizona and New Mexico to Amarillo, Texas. On April 1, she flew all the way to Harrisburg, Pennsylvania, refueling in Oklahoma, Illinois, and Ohio on the way. The weather changed for the worse, and on April 2, she was able to fly only a short distance to New Cumberland, Pennsylvania.

The next morning, Sharp taxied down the runway and lifted off for what would become her final flight. The Lightning had a reputation for losing an engine on takeoff—a pilot's worst nightmare. Unfortunately, Sharp's nightmare came true. The ground crew saw smoke pouring from her left engine. She barely had enough height to avoid hitting the tower. Most likely, Sharp knew she was in trouble. She altered her course to avoid crashing in a residential area. Soon after takeoff, the plane crashed in a "pancake landing."

Although the plane did not dive into the ground, the impact drove the front (nose) wheel up through the cockpit. The force broke the straps of Sharp's harness and sent her bursting through the canopy. She died instantly.

Because the WAFS had never been made part of the military, Sharp's family received no death benefits. Nancy Harkness Love asked another member of the WAFS, Nancy Batson, to accompany Sharp's body from Harrisburg back to Ord, Nebraska. With her, Batson carried $200 collected from fellow WAFS to give to Sharp's family.

It seemed that the whole town of Ord turned out for Sharp's funeral on Easter Sunday, April 9, 1944. One man, his eyes brimming with tears, asked Batson if he could drape Sharp's casket with an American flag. She agreed. The citizens of Ord would not let Sharp's sacrifice go unnoticed. On September 12, 1948, thousands of people came to honor her at the dedication of Ord Municipal Airport as Evelyn Sharp Field. A monument holding a three-bladed propeller from a P-38 stood over a concrete pyramid holding memorabilia from Sharp's flying career. During the ceremony, members of the Nebraska Air National Guard flew overhead.

In June 1996, the first annual Evelyn Sharp Day was held in Ord. The Nebraska State Historical Society displays a collection commemorating her achievements, and she is honored as a member of Nebraska's Aviation Hall of Fame.

DOROTHY SWAIN LEWIS

On September 4, 1997, former members of the WASP, their friends, and their families, gathered in Colorado Springs, Colorado, at the United States Air Force Academy to unveil a bronze sculpture. The 4.5-foot-high (1.4 m high) statue shows a woman pilot, striding proudly forward, her eyes to the sky. The artist who created her, Dorothy "Dot" Swain Lewis, had been a WASP herself, as an instructor and a pilot. Hoping to inspire young men and women to their highest achievements, Dot designed her WASP to show that women were wonderful, inspiring, patriotic, brave, capable, and beautiful.

For Dot Swain, that trail began in Asheville, North Carolina. Born in 1915, she was the second of four children. Her mother, a gifted musician, taught Dot and her brothers and sisters to love music and art. After high school, Dot was admitted to Randolph-Macon Women's College in Lynchburg, Virginia. After graduation, she decided to move to the major center for the arts— New York City.

In January 1937, she began taking art classes. She planned to become a professional artist, creating illustrations for magazines and newspapers. Then, one summer afternoon in June 1940, she drove to her family's home in Asheville. She noticed a small yellow single-engine plane flying overhead. She stopped at the Asheville-Hendersonville Airport

The face of the new air force, Cathy de la Garza, sits in the cockpit of her F-15 Eagle jet fighter aircraft.

A WASP IN THE FAMILY

Janet Reno, whose aunt, Winifred Wood, served as a WASP, spoke at the dedication of the WASP Memorial on September 4, 1997: "Let us all follow the trail of the WASP. Let us all believe in ourselves and our capacities to do what people didn't think we could do. Let us rededicate ourselves to peace in this world, to resolving our conflicts in family, community, nation, and world without knives and guns and fists so that, fifty years from now, we can look at the trailblazers of today and say we followed some very wonderful women."[1]

Former U. S. attorney general Janet Reno (left), whose aunt was a WASP pilot, unveils a portrait painted by Dorothy Swain Lewis (right) in 2001.

and paid $4 for a half-hour flight. After that, she was hooked. She wanted not simply to ride as a passenger, but to fly the plane herself.

She decided to take flying lessons. Soon her Saturday morning lessons were the highlight of her week. In August 1940, she soloed for the first time, completing eight hours of flight time. She borrowed $150 from her sister, Betty, to pay for more flying lessons. During the summer of 1941, she flew nearly every day, accumulating forty-seven hours. In October, she passed the tests for becoming a private pilot.

Swain had planned to be an illustrator. Flying was still a hobby. But the Japanese attack on Pearl Harbor on December 7, 1941, changed the lives of all Americans. Suddenly, resources were scarce. Newspapers had trouble finding paper on which to print. The prospects for a young illustrator trying to break into the business were poor at best. Swain thought her flying ability might be of use in the country's war effort. She got a job with Piper Aircraft Company in Lock Haven, Pennsylvania, in March 1942. Her job was to make airplane parts and to deliver Piper Cub planes for the factory. By the end of the summer of 1942, she had logged more than 250 hours of flying time.

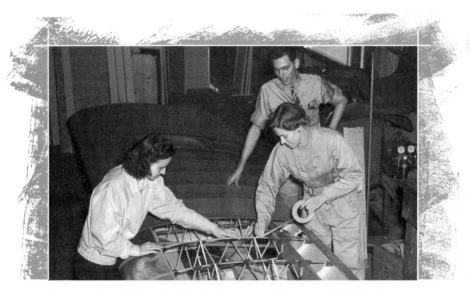

As part of an airplane familiarization course for women flight instructors at Gillespie Airfield in Nashville, Tennessee, two women trainees practice repairs to the ribs of an aircraft wing.

In September 1942, Swain's flying career took a new direction. She received a notice from Phoebe Omlie. She invited Swain to apply for the first women's aviation instruction program. Omlie had convinced the secretary of commerce that women flight instructors could train college students and military pilots. She had begun the Women's Research Flight Instructor School. Swain decided to accept the offer. She went to Gillespie Airfield in Nashville, Tennessee.

She passed her flight check easily. The course, however, would not be so easy. Beginning at 6:45 AM, she was kept busy with physical training, ground school courses, and flight instruction. By bedtime, she was exhausted. To pass the course, she needed 43 hours of flight instruction, 18 hours of solo flying, 216 hours of ground training, 18 hours of physical training, 36 hours of ground school instruction training, and 162 hours of train- ing in aviation mechanics. She graduated from the course in February 1943 and was sent to Portales, New Mexico, to teach navy seamen to fly.

Swain's students were beginning flyers. Eventually, the airmen who completed all their training would be flying off of aircraft carriers. She

At Avenger Field, women pilot trainees undergo physical conditioning. The demands of flying planes in all kinds of weather meant it was important for pilots to be in good shape.

taught four classes, stressing the "circle to the spot" landings that would enable her students to get their planes down safely on the deck of an aircraft carrier. Although she enjoyed teaching her eager airmen, she yearned to leave her little two-seater behind and pilot sleek powerful military planes. She wanted to join the WASP.

She requested an exchange from the navy program and in June 1943 became an instructor for the women's military training program, arriving in Sweetwater, Texas, for Class 43-W-8. She shared a tiny house with four other instructors. Her quarters were off-limits to students because the rules dictated that instructors and students were not to fraternize.

Technically, Swain's house, nicknamed "Ye Olde Fox Hutch" was off-limits to WASP trainees. The penalties for social interaction between students and instructors had been designed when all the instructors were men to prevent romantic relationships from developing. Although the rules seemed unnecessary when both trainees and instructors were women, they could still be enforced. Because Swain and her roommates provided one of the few social alternatives to life in the barracks, trainees were willing to risk punishment. Swain's friend and trainee, Winifred Wood, recalled a typical Saturday afternoon with Swain and her roommates. An evening with Swain was filled with good music, good food, and fun.

Although Swain enjoyed her privileges, she wanted to learn to fly the newer, more exciting planes. She resigned as a flight instructor, moved into the barracks, and became a WASP trainee. Because of her training as an instructor, she skipped ahead to Class 44-W-5, which had finished its primary flight instruction, to advanced techniques. She graduated on June 27, 1944, and was sent to twin-engine training in Columbus, Missouri. She flew engineering flight tests on the AT-10. Then she went to Laredo, Texas, to train as a copilot of the twin-engine Martin B-26. She remained in Laredo, towing targets for gunnery practice. Like Ann Baumgartner, Swain flew her planes to allow soldiers on the ground to practice firing live ammunition. The soldiers did not shoot directly at the planes but aimed at tow flags that were attached to the tail of a plane by a strong cable. In *How High She Flies*, Swain described these maneuvers:

> When I flew the B-26 Martin Marauder, we towed targets for B-24 gunners. We generally planned to meet at 6,000 feet [1,829 m], or 10,000 feet [3,048 m], a

YE OLDE FOXE HUTCH

Winifred Wood described a night at Ye Olde Fox Hutch in her book *We Were WASPS*: "There was always a good hot discussion going on over a few short ones. Someone would drag in a steak and the makings. After Jerry finished the dishes, a task which always seemed to fall to her, Dot would drag out the 'git fiddle' [guitar] and entertain us with 'Minnie from Trinidad,' 'Cocaine Bill and Morphine Sue,' and others from her large repertoire."[2]

---

predetermined altitude. We'd rendezvous with a B-26 pilot, who would join up above us. We slowed down and released a target on a cable about 400 feet [122 m] behind our aircraft. The gunners shot at those targets. The dangers, actually, weren't from wild gunners, but from the risk of mid-air collision with other B-26s.[3]

Bullets aimed at one plane flying above could hit a another plane instead.

Swain stayed on duty at Laredo Air Force Base until December 20, 1944, when the WASPs were disbanded. Suddenly, like the other WASPs around the country, she found she was no longer needed. She went back to Asheville to spend the holidays with her family and begin once again to concentrate on her art career. She received a call from Winifred Wood. She planned to write a book about the WASP and asked Swain to do the illustrations. She moved to Florida in January 1945 to work on the cartoons for the book *We Were WASPS*.

In August, Swain realized that she needed to pursue her own career. She moved once again to New York City. She found a basement apartment in Greenwich Village and began painting and illustrating greeting cards. It seemed, though, that her life was not yet ready to settle. She went to her first WASP reunion at the Piper Aircraft Company, her past employer, in Lock Haven, Pennsylvania. William T. Piper arranged for 100 new planes to be held so that the women pilots could deliver them, first to the Cleveland National Championships and then to their final destinations. Swain delivered her plane to Red Kurvin in Daytona Beach, Florida. Kurvin immediately offered her a job as an instructor in his new flight school. She also began performing in an air show. Concealed in the audience as a spectator, she would emerge as "Miss Ophelia Pratt," a schoolteacher who had taught herself to milk cows by reading a book. Miss Ophelia was sure that she could teach herself to fly the same way. After a deliberately shaky takeoff, Swain put her plane through a series of acrobatics, demonstrating that anyone can learn to fly. Anyone, that is, with more than 2,500 hours of experience.

As a flight instructor, Swain had many students thanks to the G.I. Bill, a government program designed to help returning soldiers receive education and training. The bill enabled many men to enroll in flight schools. Albert Zelius "Bert" Lewis, one of those soldiers, became Swain's student. After receiving his license, Lewis and Swain began dating and were married in June 1947. A year later, their son, Albert Jr., nicknamed "Chigger," was born. Unfortunately, after only two years of marriage Swain and Lewis divorced. Once again, Swain turned to her love of art. She taught at the Orme School in Arizona from 1951 until 1977.

A gifted sculptor, Swain had created many small statues for the WASP. In 1992, she was approached to create a WASP memorial in

At Avenger Field, women pilot trainees like this one were dunked in "The Well" when they first soloed or graduated from the program.

This memorial to WASP pilots is in the southeast courtyard of the United States Air Force Museum. The sculptor was Dorothy Swain Lewis.

Sweetwater, Texas. The sculpture stands in the center of the wishing well into which each trainee was plunged after her first successful solo flight. Another statue she made, dedicated in 1997, stands at the courtyard of the United States Air Force Museum in Colorado Springs, Colorado.

ANN BAUMGARTNER CARL

In August 1918 during World War I, Ann Baumgartner was born in an army hospital in Augusta, Georgia. Her father was serving with the armed forces in France. After her father returned from active military duty, her family moved to Plainfield, New Jersey. Ann attended Walnut Hill School in Natick, Massachusetts. At Walnut Hill School, a boarding school for girls, Baumgartner learned to be independent and to think for herself. She was encouraged to challenge herself without limits.

In this photo from 1944, British pilot Captain Joan Hughes prepares a multi-engine Hudson bomber for takeoff on a training flight. Ann Baumgartner planned to join the British Royal Air Force Transport Auxiliary before she became a WASP.

After Walnut Hill, Ann became a pre-med major in the class of 1939 at Smith College in Northhampton, Massachusetts. As graduation loomed in the near future, she could not decide on a direction for her life. She thought that a trip to Europe might help her make a choice. She left on an Italian freighter in the summer of 1939, planning to tour Spain, Sicily, and Italy before meeting her mother in England to stay with family there. On September 1, 1939, while she visited her mother's family, Hitler's armies invaded Poland. Two days later, Britain declared war on Germany.

Her relatives insisted that Baumgartner and her mother leave England as soon as possible. They left on September 2 on a ship overflowing with refugees. They were packed into a large room where fifty mattresses had been laid on the floor 6 inches (15 centimeters) apart. They were unable to change their clothes. The toilet facilities clogged and leaked onto the floor. The fear of being torpedoed and sunk during the voyage hung over the ship. Finally, they steamed past the Statue of Liberty into New York Harbor.

Back in the United States, Baumgartner found a medical research job in New Jersey, investigating the effects of vitamins that had been extracted from fish oils. At the vitamin company, she sometimes took a break by climbing to the roof for a view of the Manhattan skyline. One evening, she watched an airplane cross the sky. She imagined doing nothing but piloting that airplane across the country, looking at the world stretching away around her. She decided to take flying lessons and become a commercial pilot. Using the money she earned at her research job, she began her flying lessons and soon earned her private pilot's license. She planned to join the Royal Air Force Transport Auxiliary in England, the only wartime option available to women pilots at the time.

Hoping for an assignment flying an air ambulance, Baumgartner needed to accumulate 200 hours of flying time, the requirement for a commercial license. She and another pilot, Jasper White, bought an old Piper Cub and alternated flying. She was near her goal in the summer of 1942, when the government, having sighted submarines offshore, closed the eastern coast to all private flying. She feared that her objective would be unreachable. Then she heard a news story about the WASP. The army was looking for experienced women pilots to fly noncombat missions in

Women ferry pilots take a break at Houston Municipal Airport before picking up their aircraft and flying assignments.

the United States. Baumgartner met with
Jacqueline Cochran in her Manhattan apartment
late in 1942. Shortly before Christmas,
Baumgartner received orders to report to Houston,
Texas, in January 1943 as part of the WASP Class
of 1943—W3.

As Baumgartner rode the train to Houston,
she pictured life on an active air force base with
dozens of shining, sleek silver planes lined up
along runways busy with incoming and outgoing
air traffic. In reality, Jacqueline Cochran had not
yet found a permanent home for the first recruits
in her program. Anxious to get started, she had set
up at the end of a runway on the Houston
Municipal Airport. There was no mess hall, no
barracks, no infirmary—and no bathroom! When
necessary, trainees had to walk all the way to the
main terminal building. No shiny silver planes
shimmered in the sunlight. Instead, Baumgartner
found old Piper Cubs.

Baumgartner and the other recruits were housed
in hotels in town, which seemed acceptable until
they were assigned to their rooms. Two women were
assigned to each room, but the room had only one
bed. They would be paid $150 a month and be
expected to pay for their own meals. Baumgartner

A WASP trainee received instruction in radio operations, one of the many skills required by pilots. Radios were used for navigation as well as communication.

took ground school courses—navigation, meteorology, and Morse code. She learned how an engine works by taking it apart and rebuilding it.

Then one evening, her dream of "real" flight training came true. Air force fighter planes—PT-19s and BT-13s—arrived, sleek and shiny. In the PT-19s, Baumgartner flew cross-country flights, careful to keep the navigation charts from blowing out of its open cockpit. The BT-13 had a canopy over the cockpit and was heavier and more powerful.

Baumgartner spent fifty-five hours in the PT-19 and sixty-five hours in the BT-13. She flew other planes, too, practicing flying with and without instruments. She passed her flight and ground school tests and graduated on September 11, 1943. Her first assignment was to a tow-target squadron of the Artillery Base at Camp Davis in North Carolina. She would replace a woman who had been killed when her plane crashed.

Baumgartner's mission was to help artillery gunners train. She towed a cloth target behind her airplane. The gunners shot at the target with live ammunition. Although they were not aiming at the planes, many planes returned with bullet holes in them. After all, these men were just learning how to fire their guns. She also flew back and forth to test radar tracking by the gunner trainees. She flew at night, too. She flew different patterns at varying altitudes while the trainees tried to track her with searchlights. This mission also gave her an opportunity to build up a lot of flying hours. Plus, during her free time, she was encouraged to take cross-country flights to practice her navigational skills.

A common assignment for WASP pilots was target towing, so that combat pilots could practice their gunnery skills. Here, a WASP pilot in an A-24 Douglas dive bomber tows a target as a woman pilot looks on from another aircraft.

Part of WASP training, as for all other military pilots, involved time in a high-altitude chamber, where they became familiar with the physiological effects of reduced atmospheric pressure.

In February 1944, Baumgartner and Betty Greene, another member of the WASP, were sent to Wright Field in Dayton, Ohio, to test high-altitude and low-temperature equipment. Wright Field was a research facility where scientists studied the effects of high-altitude flying, oxygen deprivation, and gravitational forces on the human body. Baumgartner and Greene were assigned to partici-pate for about a week. They worked with Dr. Alice

TEST PILOTS

What did a pilot test? First, as manufacturers produced new plane models they had to be tested and accepted by the air force. Did the plane perform to the manufacturer's specifications? Then pilots tested fuels to see which helped the plane perform best. When engineers designed new engine parts or propellers, pilots checked to see if the planes flew faster and more safely with the new parts. Because new equipment sometimes made the plane unpredictable, test flying was dangerous.

Brues to design the best possible flying suit. They wore different clothing so that the results could be compared. They tested clothing for warmth and flexibility. Was an alpaca-lined suit warm enough or too bulky? Should zippers be zipped up or left opened? Would muddy boots slip when pilots climbed on the wing to get into the cockpit? Even underwear and socks were tested.

Once the tests were over, Baumgartner returned to target flying at Davis Field. Two weeks later, though, she was packing again. In

March 1944, her request for a transfer had been approved. She was going back to Wright Field as part of the Fighter Flight Test Branch. She was not going to test clothing, though. This time she would be testing the planes.

Usually the purpose of her flight was to test the plane itself or its parts—instruments, engine parts, or overall performance. On one occasion, though, Baumgartner flew a P-51 to test a new gunsight. She flew to a target on the eastern tip of an island in Lake Erie. She made several high-speed passes, shooting the guns at the target. Since women were not allowed to fly combat missions, Baumgartner was most likely the only WASP to shoot a fighter plane's guns during WWII.

Baumgartner not only tested fighter planes, she also tested bombers. Two tests, both involving long-range flights, were especially important. The first was a test to refuel the bomber from another plane in midair, without landing. The second part of the test involved carrying a heavy load for many hours. The load weighed 8,900 pounds (4,037 kg) and filled an area 10 feet (3 m) by 28 inches (71 cm). After the war, she would understand that she had been testing the B-29, the type of plane that would drop the atomic bomb.

In October 1944, Baumgartner made history again. The United States had been working on a new plane that would be powered by a jet-fueled engine. The plane was ready for testing, but the United States government wanted secrecy. When the YP-59A arrived at Wright Field, it had a false propeller so no one could tell that it was a jet. Once the jet was fired up for the test flight, the distinctive jet noise told the world what made the fighter fly.

THE ATOMIC BOMB

At 2:00 AM on August 6, 1945, the *Enola Gay*, a B-59 bomber, took off toward Japan. At 8:09, the crew could see the city of Hiroshima as they cruised 26,000 feet [7,925 m] above. At 8:16, the first atomic bomb, "Little Boy," was released, causing a terrible, unimaginably strong explosion, the equivalent of 20,000 tons [18,144 metric tons] of TNT. On the ground, approximately 80,000 people died in the blast. A second atomic bomb was dropped on the city of Nagasaki three days later.

Baumgartner's job during the test flight was to compare the speed, stability, and handling of the jet to that of other fighters. It turned out to have a stability problem that forced Baumgartner to correct the course. Adjustments would need to be made before the plane could be put into production

At the same time, she heard some disturbing news. The WASP would be disbanded in December. Between October and December 1944, she was given permission to fly in most of the planes she had not had a chance to try. She also tested a newly designed plane. Two P-51 plane fuselages were put together separated by a wind section. The plane had two cockpits, one in each fuselage. The plane had been designed by an air force major named Bill Carl. The design turned out to be a success, as did the relationship between Baumgartner and Carl. They were married on May 12, 1945, five months after the WASP disbanded.

They lived first in Virginia, then moved to Long Island, New York, in 1945, where Carl designed and built hydrofoil boats for the navy. He formed Dynamic Developments, Inc., a company that was eventually bought by Grumman Aerospace. He and Baumgartner had two children. After they were in school, Baumgartner went back to flying as an instructor and as a pilot for Dynamic Developments, Inc.

Baumgartner never got over her love of adventure. In 1977, after Carl retired from Grumman, he and Baumgartner sold everything, including their house and cars, and bought a 45-foot (14 m) sailing yacht. They spent the next two years sailing to Bermuda, Canada, Europe, throughout the Mediterranean, and the Caribbean. Baumgartner wrote a book about her adventures: *The Small World of Long-Distance Sailors.*

THE FLIGHT HOME

The WASP were not the only women who had joined the war effort and would soon be sent home. Many women had become part of the civilian labor force. "Rosie the Riveter" was the symbol for women who gave up housework to build airplanes. Between 1940 and 1944, the number of women employed in war-related industries had risen 460 percent, and female membership in labor unions had quadrupled. In 1942, at the Kaiser Shipyard in Portland, Oregon, women made up 60 percent of the workforce. But as the war was winding down, some people began to worry. Would the women go

A woman machinist helps to build an aircraft engine in 1943. Many women took skilled machinist jobs during the war.

Eleanor Roosevelt, wife of President Franklin D. Roosevelt, encouraged women to play a more decisive role in the war effort and took a personal interest in the WASP program.

home? In the summer of 1944, the War Department published a pamphlet called *Do You Want Your Wife to Work After the War?* The pamphlet spoke against women working. As soldiers began returning home, the image of working women as comrades-in-arms was replaced by the danger of women competing with men. Women should be delighted to give up their jobs and return to their proper place—the kitchen. All of a sudden, newspapers and magazines, even those designed for women, like *Ladies Home Journal*, gave women a clear message: Go home! Articles appeared linking juvenile delinquency to the absence of a mother at home.

First Lady Eleanor Roosevelt tried to counter these stories. The country could not afford to return, she warned, to an economy in which women were denied the right to work. Unfortunately, most men did not agree. The military establishment was well aware that training male pilots to replace the more experienced WASP would take $1 million and four months. In the meantime, airplanes, especially pursuit planes, would sit on runways.

Besides, the WASP wanted to stay. Some of them had just finished training. They could continue to serve their country only if they signed on for non-flying duty. About 155 WASP made that choice. Even when ferrying commanders asked if their WASP pilots could stay, the army sent them home.

They were sent home, but they had to pay their own way. Some WASP applied for jobs as commercial airline pilots. But the only jobs available to women were as flight attendants. Some found jobs as flight instructors, but for many flying was too expensive or too difficult to arrange. Many never flew again, returning to their lives as housewives and mothers, the expected role of women in the 1940s. Others got jobs in the aviation industry but did not fly planes.

The WASP had been a well-kept secret. For decades, history ignored their contribution to the Allies' success. Then in 1976, the U.S. Air Force declared that women would begin pilot training. These would be the first women to fly United

States military aircraft. The WASP were angry. They had been the first women to fly planes for the military. Their years of service were once again being ignored. They decided to repeat the actions that had sent them home in 1944. They organized a publicity campaign. Senator Barry Goldwater sponsored a new bill in Congress that would finally give the WASP military status. WASP

around the country asked people to sign petitions supporting the bill. They spoke to news reporters and government officials. On November 23, 1977, the WASP bill passed and was signed into law by President Jimmy Carter.

Below, members of the last graduating class of the WASP sit for a class portrait.

In 1977, President Jimmy Carter signed a bill giving the WASP full military status.

In 1987, Brigadier General Wilma Vaught began raising money for a memorial to recognize the military service of women. On October 18, 1997, the Women in Military Service for America Memorial was dedicated. The memorial, located at the entrance to Arlington National Cemetery in Washington, D.C., is America's first major national memorial honoring women who have served in all branches of the armed forces throughout the nation's history.

Because the WASP received veteran status in 1977, Julie Englund, dean for administration at Harvard Law School, assumed that her mother, Irene, was entitled to a funeral at Arlington National Cemetery. Englund's father, a navy lieutenant, had been honored with this ceremony when he died in 1996. She was shocked to discover that military policy excluded her mother.

Following the example of former WASP, she began a publicity campaign, writing newspaper editorials on behalf of all surviving WASP. Her campaign worked. Irene Englund became the first WASP to receive burial with honors, complete with a rifle salute, at Arlington.

Shown at left is an American Victory Medal, which was awarded to all WASP. At right is an American Campaign Medal, which was awarded in 1977 to all WASP who had served for more than a year.

In this photo from 1946, Jacqueline Cochran stands beside a fighter plane that she has painted with a special message to promote women's participation in military aviation.

Finally, it seemed, women pilots who had sacrificed for their country during World War II would get the recognition they deserved.

TIMELINE

December 3, 1938	Jacqueline Cochran wins the Bendix International Air Race.
July 1941	Jacqueline Cochran submits a plan for a women's air corps to General Hap Arnold.
December 7, 1941	Japan attacks the American naval base at Pearl Harbor, and the United States declares war.
December 11, 1941	Germany declares war on the United States.
October 19, 1942	Seven women, including Nancy Love, graduate from the Women's Auxiliary Ferrying Squadron and begin ferrying airplanes.
January 27, 1943	First bombing raid by American aircraft on Germany takes place at Wilhemshaven.
May 1943	German and Italian troops surrender in North Africa.
June 6, 1944	American forces land on the beaches of Normandy.
August 25, 1944	Paris is liberated by Allied forces.
October 1944	There are now 130 women pilots in the WASP program, ferrying two-thirds of all pursuit and fighter aircraft manufactured in the United States.
December 1944	The Women Airforce Service Pilots program is disbanded.
February 14, 1945	The German city of Dresden is destroyed by firebombing.
April 21, 1945	Soviet troops reach the outskirts of Berlin.
April 30, 1945	Adolf Hitler commits suicide.

August 6, 1945	The atomic bomb is dropped on Hiroshima.
August 14, 1945	The Japanese agree to an unconditional surrender.
1953	Jacqueline Cochran becomes the first woman pilot to fly faster than the speed of sound.
1977	President Jimmy Carter signs a bill honoring the members of the Women Airforce Service Pilots and granting them military status.

Glossary

barnstormer A pilot who performed acrobatics in the air, like wing-walking or parachute jumping. They were called barnstormers because they needed a farmer's field or pasture from which to stage their shows.

canopy The glass or plastic cover of the pilot's compartment, including the windscreen.

G.I. Bill Passed in 1944, this bill provided financial assistance for education and training, loan guarantees for homes and farms, and job placement assistance to soldiers released from military service.

Great Depression The worst economic collapse in the world, it lasted from 1929 until the early 1940s. Banks and business closed, leaving 15 million Americans, nearly one-quarter of the workforce, without jobs.

militarization Of great importance to the WASP, it would have given insurance benefits to the women pilots and made them veterans eligible for the provisions of the G.I. Bill.

war rationing During World War II, American citizens were allowed to purchase only a specific amount of items like food and gasoline. Supplying the troops was considered more important.

Women's Auxiliary Army Corps (WAAC)
Created in 1942, the WAAC filled noncombat jobs with women, freeing men for active service in combat. Initially, the women were hired as civilian employees. In 1943, the word "Auxiliary" was dropped and the WAC became part of the military.

Works Progress Administration (WPA) A government work program that gave people jobs that helped the public, like building bridges, roads, and public parks.

For More Information

Air Force Museum Foundation
P.O. Box 1903
1100 Spatz Street
Wright-Patterson AFB, Ohio 45433-7102
(937) 255-3286

American Airpower Heritage Museum
Midland International Airport
9600 Wright Drive
Midland, TX 79711
Web site: http://www.airpowermuseum.org

National Aviation Hall of Fame
P.O. Box 31096
Dayton, OH 45437
Web site: http://www.nationalaviation.org/

United States Air Force Academic Library
2354 Fairchild Drive, Suite 3A10
USAF Academy, CO 80840-6214
(719) 333-2590

The Women's Museum
3800 Parry Avenue
Dallas, TX 75226
(214) 915-0860
Web site: http://www.thewomensmuseum.org

WEB SITES
Due to the changing nature of Internet links, the Rosen Publishing Group, Inc., has developed an online list of Web sites related to the subject of this book. This site is updated regularly. Please use this link to access the list:

http://www.rosenlinks.com/aww/wpww

For Further Reading

Bartels, Diane Ruth Armour. *Sharpie: The Life Story of Evelyn Sharp*. Lincoln, NE: Dageforde Publishing, 1996.

Carl, Ann B. *A WASP Among Eagles: A Military Test Pilot in World War II*. Washington, DC: Smithsonian Institution, 1999.

Cochran, Jacqueline. *Jackie Cochran: The Autobiography of the Greatest Woman Pilot in Aviation History*. New York: Bantam, 1987.

Cole, Jean Hascall. *Women Pilots of World War II*. Salt Lake City: University of Utah Press, 2002.

Cooper, Ann L. *How High She Flies: Dorothy Swain Lewis*. Arlington Heights, IL: Aviatrix Publishing, 1999.

Keil, Sally Van Wagenen. *Those Wonderful Women in Their Flying Machines: The Unknown Heroines of World War II*. New York: Four Directions Press, 1979.

Nathan, Amy. *Yankee Doodle Gals: Women Pilots of World War II*. Washington, DC: National Geographic, 2001.

Rickman. Sarah Byrn. *The Originals: Women's Auxiliary Ferrying Squadron of World War II*. Sarasota, FL: Discus Books, 2001.

Bibliography

Bartels, Diane Ruth Armour. *Sharpie: The Life Story of Evelyn Sharp.* Lincoln, NE: Dageforde Publishing, 1996.

Carl, Ann B. *A WASP Among Eagles: A Military Test Pilot in World War II.* Washington, DC: Smithsonian Institution, 1999.

Cochran, Jacqueline. *The Stars at Noon.* Boston: Little Brown, 1954.

Cochran, Jaqueline. *Jackie Cochran: The Autobiography of the Greatest Woman Pilot in Aviation History.* New York: Bantam, 1987.

Cole, Jean Hascall. "An Oral History: Self Interview." *Women Airforce Service Pilots Oral History Project.* The Women's Collection, Texas Women's University, 2003. Retrieved September 25, 2003 (http://www.twu.edu/wasp/cole2.pdf).

Cooper, Ann L. *How High She Flies: Dorothy Swain Lewis.* Arlington Heights, IL: Aviatrix Publishing, 1999.

Source Notes

Chapter 4
1. Sarah Byrn Rickman, *The Originals: The Women's Auxiliary Ferrying Squadron of World War II*, (Sarasota, FL: Discus Books), p. 64.

Chapter 5
1. Winifred Wood and Dorothy Swain Lewis, *We Were WASPs* (Coral Gables, FL: Glade House, 1945), p. 44.
2. Ibid., p. 193.
3. Ann L. Cooper, *How High She Flies: Dorothy Swain Lewis* (Arlington Heights, IL: Aviatrix Publishing, 1999), p. 87.

Index

About the Author

Karen Donnelly is the author of many books for the Rosen Publishing Group, including *Everything You Need to Know About Lyme Disease,* Cruzan v. Missouri: *The Right to Die,* and *Football Hall of Famers: Deacon Jones.*

Photo Credits

Front and back cover, p. 97 WASP WWII Museum, http://www.avengerfield.org; p. 5 © Corbis; pp. 6, 27, 38, 92, 98 © Bettmann/Corbis; pp. 11, 20, 36, 39, 48, 51, 55, 56, 67, 73, 79, 81, 83, 84, 94–95 Woman's Collection, Texas Woman's University; pp. 16, 18, 31, 58 Culver Pictures; pp. 32, 42, 63, 64 © AP/Wide World Photos; p. 66 Gillespie Aviation Collection, Photo 53, Albert Gore Research Center, MTSU; p. 74 WASP Memorial at the United States Air Force Museum; p. 76 © Hulton-Deutsch Collection/Corbis; p. 91 © Hulton Archive/Getty Images; p. 96 © Wally McNamee/Corbis.

Designer: Evelyn Horovicz; **Editor:** Jake Goldberg; **Photo Researcher:** Peter Tomlinson

DATE DUE

PRINTED IN U.S.A.

GAYLORD